Adult Coloring Book

An Adult Coloring Book Featuring Uplifting and
Inspirational Phrases for Stress Relief and Relaxation

PUBLISHED BY THE FRUITFUL MIND LTD.

COLORING BOOK
Cafe

Disclaimer

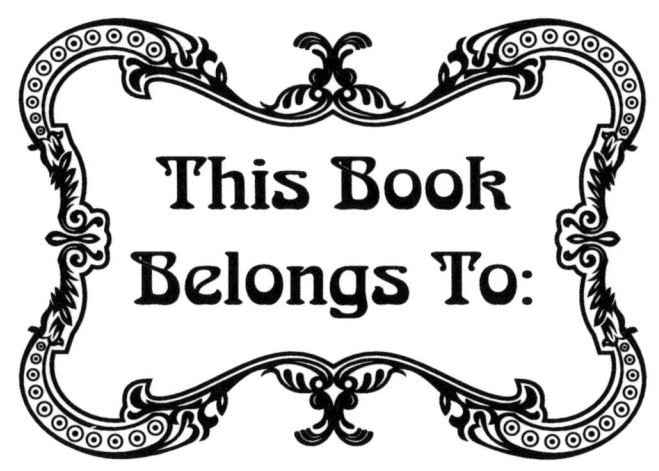

This Book
Belongs To:

BONUS

Relax And Create Your Own Masterpiece With
THIS 30 PAGE FREE *Beautiful Adult Coloring Book*

Claim Your FREE Coloring Book at:

www.freecoloringbooklet.com

Samples Below

Better an oops than a what if

Where Life plants you bloom with Grace

Be happy
Be bright
Be you

Do more of what makes you happy

Printed in Great Britain
by Amazon